Geranium Morning

D1294509

Geranium Morning

by E. Sandy Powell

illustrations by
Renée Graef

A BOOK ABOUT

GRIEF

CAROLRHODA BOOKS

MINNEAPOLIS, MINNESOTA   USA

This book is available in two editions:
Library binding by Carolrhoda Books, Inc.
Soft cover by First Avenue Editions
c/o The Lerner Group
241 First Avenue North
Minneapolis, Minnesota 55401

Library of Congress Cataloging-in-Publication Data

Powell, E. Sandy.
  Geranium morning / by E. Sandy Powell; illustrations by Renée
Graef.
    p.   cm.
  Summary: Two friends who lose parents, one suddenly in an
accident and one by illness, learn to deal with their grief.
  ISBN 0-87614-380-X (lib. bdg.)
  ISBN 0-87614-542-X (pbk.)
  1. Children and death—Juvenile literature. 2. Parents—Death—
Psychological aspects—Juvenile literature. 3. Bereavement in
children—Juvenile literature. 4. Parent and child—Juvenile
literature. [1. Death. 2. Parent and child.] I. Graef, Renée, ill.
II. Title.
BF723.D3P68   1990
155.9′37—dc20   89-33539

Manufactured in the United States of America
3 4 5 6 7 8 – P/SF – 01 00 99 98 97 96

To LeAnn

I have the same name as my dad—Timothy Brandon Blair. But ever since Dad died, nothing's been the same.

Dad used to leave work early to take care of me after school. Mom works in an office and can't come home early. Now I take care of myself.

Dad used to take me on outings. I loved the reptile house at the zoo. Dad liked going to the arboretum. Now when I go out, I see other kids with their dads. I hate not having my dad anymore.

I'm glad about one thing though. I have a new friend. Her name is Frannie, and she understands.

Frannie knows my secrets, like how I couldn't sleep in on Saturdays because I had nightmares of my last morning with Dad. I can still see him poking his head in my room.

"Want to come to the nursery?" he asked. "It's time to get my geraniums."

Once each spring, Dad added to his collection. Our porch was full of planters. The planters were full of geraniums. I thought he should get a new hobby, but Dad said, "Geranium morning's a family tradition!"

I hoped he'd go on without me this year, so I scrunched down in bed. I said I was tired, even though I wasn't. Really, I didn't want to wait around while he picked out the plants. And I especially didn't want to ride home balancing those pots on my lap. Geraniums smell funny, sort of like sour old pennies. Dad liked the smell because it reminded him of his grandfather.

My friend Frannie knows my other secret too—why I can't stand cocoa. That morning I told Dad, "I'll be up for cocoa when you get home." Mom always made cocoa on geranium mornings.

"All right," he said. "I'll miss you. See you when I get home."

But he never did. Maybe "I'll miss you" was the last thing he said. I can't quite remember.

I do remember Mom screaming when I came down for cocoa. I thought Dad would be home any minute. I didn't know the police had just left.

That was the worst morning of my life! Right away my relatives came. Before I could ask any questions, my aunt hurried all the kids outside to play. I didn't want to play! I wanted somebody to tell me what was going on. I wanted to see my dad.

Finally Mom called me into the kitchen and told me what happened. "A man was driving his truck the wrong way. Your dad didn't see it in time. He was killed."

Mom started crying and reached out to hug me. I didn't mean to pull away. I thought I was going to throw up.

I wish I'd known Frannie then. Even with people all around, I felt so alone. For weeks my relatives tried to cheer me up. I didn't want to go to the zoo or any other place I had been to with Dad. But I didn't want to be left alone either, especially on Saturday mornings.

Mom quit cooking, so we ran out for burgers almost every night. I never thought I could get sick of hamburgers! I tried to cook, but my macaroni tasted even worse.

Mom yelled at me a lot—whenever I made even little mistakes. Didn't she know it was hard on me too? After all, I am just a kid. Maybe she wished it'd been me instead of Dad. Maybe if I'd been there to hold the geraniums...

Nobody understood how I felt. But then, I didn't understand myself either. I'd be sad one minute, mad the next, then I'd be laughing out of control. It seemed like my old friends didn't like me anymore. And my teachers made me nervous. They said I needed discipline, like the school bully, Jeremiah Turkle. But I wasn't like Jeremiah! Things just bothered me more than they used to, and sometimes that got me in trouble.

One day after school, Jeremiah made me really mad. But it turned out all right because that's how I met Frannie.

Jeremiah was shooting spitballs at some girls. Frannie, who'd just transferred to our school, didn't see him and came walking by. Jeremiah leaped out in front of her and wouldn't let her pass. I hadn't met Frannie yet, so I didn't know if she could defend herself. But I knew Jeremiah hurt people, and I didn't like people getting hurt.

"Stop it!" I hollered.

Jeremiah wouldn't stop. Instead he tugged on her sweater. Without even thinking about how big he was, I grabbed Jeremiah's shirt and spun him around. He fell into the dirt. That surprised everybody! But then a teacher came around the side of the building, and we all took off.

Frannie said thanks as we ran across the playground.

"Sure," I said, following her through the gate. I liked being a hero.

Then she surprised me. "Your dad died last year, didn't he?"

I couldn't believe she said that after I'd just helped her.

"None of your business!"

"I know it's none of my business," she apologized. "A teacher told me about your dad. My mom is dying."

I wasn't expecting that either.

"I'm sorry." What was I supposed to say to a girl whose mother was dying? "I'm really sorry," I said again. I meant it.

My stomach felt awful, and I couldn't swallow. I wanted to leave her there, but I heard myself saying, "I'll walk you home." I didn't talk to her though. I was glad when we got to her house.

"Well, see you later," I didn't know what else to say.

"Want to come in for some juice?"

"No thanks." I hung my head.

"It's my mom, isn't it?"

She looked hurt. I couldn't answer.

"I thought you'd understand!" she cried. The door slammed behind her.

I felt about as small as the ants I stepped over on my way down the walk.

The next day whenever I saw Frannie, she wouldn't look at me. I wanted to forget about her, but I couldn't. Finally after school, I went to talk to her.

"I'm sorry," I said.

"It's all right."

She didn't look all right though. She looked sad.

"I guess I was scared," I said. "I've never known anyone who's dying. It made me think of my dad."

"Do you still miss him?"

"Yeah." I was beginning to like Frannie.

"Want to come over now?" she asked.

"Sure. I just need to call my mom from your house."

We talked while we walked. She asked me if I was still scared to meet her mom.

"Well," I said, "maybe a little. I know this sounds dumb, but does your mom have a disease that other people can catch?"

"No," Frannie answered. "I used to wonder that too, until I asked my dad. It's something hardly anybody gets. And it's something the doctors can't fix. Mom says we just have to be brave."

I had another lump in my throat, but I didn't feel scared anymore. We raced to Frannie's house.

When we went into the living room, Frannie's mom was lying on the couch. She looked tired and a little bit boney. I liked her voice though. It sounded scratchy but soft. I felt fine with Frannie's mom.

My mom liked having Frannie around too. She even started cooking again. Sometimes Frannie came over for dinner. When Mom had a meeting, I'd stay late at Frannie's. Her mom and dad would play games with us.

Then, just when things seemed to be going so well, Frannie's mom got worse. For days Frannie and I didn't play together. Frannie would go right home after school. One morning she didn't come to school at all. My teacher told us that Frannie's mother had died.

I couldn't pay attention in class. As soon as the last bell rang, I ran right to Frannie's house. Lots of people were standing around. Frannie was curled up on the couch.

"I'm sorry I couldn't call you," she said, "but I'm glad you're here."

I knew exactly how Frannie felt. I sat next to her on the couch all afternoon.

The days after that are kind of a blur. Frannie and I were always together, except on Thursday nights. She had joined a counseling group.

"They're all kids like us," she said. "We talk to each other about how we feel. Why don't you come with me?"

"No," I said. "Mom wouldn't let me. She says we've got to get on with our lives."

Frannie disagreed. "My dad says it takes a long time to settle things inside yourself."

Frannie seemed smarter than me.

Then all of a sudden she was crying. I didn't mind. When she stopped, I tried to make her feel better. "At least you got to say good-bye."

"Yeah, but I had to watch her go."

I thought hard about that. I didn't know which was worse.

Frannie was sniffling again. I wondered if I should be quiet, but I couldn't stop myself.

"You know what bothers me the most?" I asked. "The 'if onlys'—'If only I'd gone with Dad. I know I would've seen the truck in time' or 'if only he hadn't wanted more of those stinking geraniums!'"

Frannie looked at me. "'If onlys' won't bring him back."

She was right.

I don't know how Frannie and I would have made it alone. The sadness didn't go away, but knowing that we had each other helped.

The weeks faded into months. Frannie's dad took us out a lot—more hamburgers! And on Saturday mornings Mom let Frannie come over.

Last Saturday, though, I slept in—for the first time since Dad died. When I woke up I called Frannie.

"Want to come to the nursery with me?"

"Geranium morning?" she asked.

"Yes. I have something to settle." It was time to get Dad's geraniums.

ABOUT THE AUTHOR

E. Sandy Powell lives with her three children and their many pets in Camas, Washington. She earned her B.A. degree in education, with a specialty in learning facilitation in a changing world, graduating with honors from Western Washington University. Ms. Powell has worked for years in child care, preschool education, and teaching. Now she spends half her day working as a freelance writer.

ABOUT THE ARTIST

Renée Graef received a bachelor of science degree in art from the University of Wisconsin, in Madison, in 1980. She still lives in Madison and now works as an illustrator. One of her favorite pastimes is hiking in the woods. When she's not hiking or drawing, Ms. Graef can probably be found adding to her collection of about 140 women's hats.